Johnny Appleseed

For my wonderful nieces—
Megan, Sarah, and Anastasia
—P.D.

For my mother and Morgan
—M.M.

ISBN 0-439-13325-4

12 11 10 9 8 7 6 5 4 3 2 1   9/9 0 1 2 3 4/0

Printed in the U.S.A.   24

First Scholastic printing, September 1999

B'day - Sept. 26, 1774 born in Mass.

(Went out West through the wilderness 200 yrs ago.

traveled out West - Mainly Penn., Ohio establishing apple orchards.

- folktale - story that has been passed down & told many times

Johnny

He became an Amer. Hero & his story told over & over.

Appleseed

Nova, Ohio - is home to a 176 yr. old tree, the last known to be planted by him.

By Patricia Demuth

Illustrated by Michael Montgomery

He supplied apple seeds to settlers in the middle Western Great Lakes area. He was a very generous person & would often give the struggling pioneers seedlings for free

- He wore a coffee sack, tin hat & traveled barefoot.

* This is how he got his name "Johnny Appleseed"

true / fiction

SCHOLASTIC INC.
New York Toronto London Auckland Sydney
Mexico City New Delhi Hong Kong

for his kindness to the pioneers

Who was Johnny Appleseed?
Was he just in stories?
No.
Johnny was a real person.
His name was John Chapman.
He planted apple trees—
lots and lots of them.
So people called him
Johnny Appleseed.

Johnny was young
when our country was young.
Back then many people
were moving West.

There were no towns,
no schools,
not even many houses.
And there were no apple trees.
None at all.

Johnny was going West, too.
He wanted to plant apple trees.
He wanted to make the West
a nicer place to live.
So Johnny got a big, big bag.
He filled it with apple seeds.

Then he set out.

Johnny walked for days
and weeks.
On and on.
Soon his clothes were rags.
His feet were bare.
And what kind of hat
did he wear?
A cooking pot!
That way he didn't
have to carry it.

Snow came.

Did Johnny stop?

No.

He made snowshoes.
Then he walked
some more.

Spring came.

Johnny was out West now.

He stopped by a river.

He dug a hole.

Inside he put an apple seed.

Then he covered it with dirt.

Someday an apple tree
would stand here.
Johnny set out again.
He had lots more
seeds to plant.

Johnny walked by himself.
But he was not alone.

The animals were his friends.

Most people were afraid
of wild animals.
They had guns to shoot them.
But not Johnny.
One day a big, black bear
saw Johnny go by.
It did not hurt Johnny.
Maybe the bear knew
Johnny was a friend.

The Indians were
Johnny's friends, too.

They showed him how to find
good food—
berries and plants and roots.

Where did Johnny sleep?

Under the stars.

Johnny liked to lie on his back
and look up.

The wind blew softly.

Owls hooted.

The stars winked down at him.

Many years passed.
Johnny planted apple trees
everywhere.
People started to call him
Johnny Appleseed.

One day he came back to where
he had planted the first seed.
It was a big tree now.
A girl was swinging in it.

That night Johnny stayed
with the girl's family.
He told stories.
Everybody liked Johnny.
"Stay with us," they said.
"Make a home here."

But Johnny did not stay.
"I have work to do,"
he said.
"I am happy.
The whole world
is my home."

More and more people
came out West.
Johnny planted
more and more trees.
In the spring, the trees bloomed
with white flowers.

In the fall,
there were apples—
red, round, ripe apples.

People made apple pies.
And apple butter for their bread.

And apple cider to drink.
And children had apple trees
to climb.

It was all thanks
to Johnny Appleseed.